Kolayah-KeeVan

Only
1
Will Speak

Only 1 Will Speak / Kolayah-KeeVan
109 pages 6" x 9", perfect binding, cream interior paper (60# weight),
black and white interior ink, white exterior paper (100# weight),
full-color exterior ink.

Language: English
Country: United States

Forward by Shaun Judah
Edited by Tina Tatum

ISBN 978-0-6151-8452-4

Forward

Kolayah-KeeVan Wilson is simply an inspiration, as a writer, as a poet, as a man.

To often we come into contact with those whom we seldom get to understand, Kolayah is not one of those individuals. In our one face -to-face meeting, 1 was fortunate enough to meet a calm spirit so full of life that his quiet demeanor scared me. The Power with which his subdued voice spoke exuded so many more things than just a male human, he speaks as he is a Spirit.

From the humbling "And They All Can Refresh" to the romantically sweet "A Sunday Afternoon" Kolayah captures the reader with an inherent purpose to make you think outside of the box. The stories and poems of "<u>Only 1 Will Speak</u>" capture the thoughts and emotions of the millions of souls scattered across the earth in the harmony of 1 voice.

The perception of this husband, father, friend, and writer comes through in a resounding whisper, we are all the same.

Shaun Judah

Dedication

This poetic expression of life is dedicated to The Creator off <u>ALL</u>, my wife; La Shawn, children; Qumran and Kaiyah, my Mom and Dad; Dot and Ray Wilson, Visionaire, all of my poet, writer and author Brothers and Sisters that are walking in their calling and bringing relevant vision and literary art to the world.

Preface

As beings we strive to find the meaning of it all. In doing so we validate self. We BECOME. As writers, poets, speakers, educators, parents, children, siblings, family, preachers, ministers, prophets, sinners, saints, seekers, photographers, directors and peeps, we constantly are looking for ways to better receive and convey wisdom. So, I question you, are there really that many ways of doing so?

In that spark of wisdom that we receive, we are expressing that one thread of wisdom as we live and share similar visions in diverse ways according to our many concepts, beliefs, enlightenments, consciousness', experiences and growth; all to get that perfect way of conveying our total life experience. This is oneness at its best. As I have so lovingly shared before, we are universal, one verse, one voice.

Only I Will Speak; from front cover to back cover, is an entanglement of my life experiences and the one wise thought that has been expressed, rewritten and re lived in many forms that allow me to BECOME.

The journey is not complete. Does it just end or do we continue to be?

Take this journey with me until begin being becomes.

Kolayah-KeeVan Wilson

Table Of Contents
Only 1 Will Speak
by Kolayah-KeeVan

Table Of Contents
Only 1 Will Speak
by Kolayah-KeeVan

Table Of Contents
Only 1 Will Speak
by Kolayah-KeeVan

Only 1 Will Speak

Only 1 Will Speak

I don't have thoughts in my head
there are people
staying up all night talking to me
and arguing
when I need to sleep
why are they more vocal after sundown
in the morning they're silent

I don't have thoughts in my head
there are People
ARGUING
I Need Sleep
They're more vocal after sundown
in the morning only 1 will speak

Literary Artist

Literary Artist

They call me a Literary Artist
because I paint with my words
one stroke of my pen
and colorful worlds explode

My mouth creates the Story Boards
that become vivid motion pictures
in your imagination
with vicarious gazes

Like children on summer vacation
gaping mouths
eyes wide seeing the preview
of the summer blockbuster

Pulling out your imaginary sword
screaming
I am Captain Jack Sparrow
then laughing like a child

And They All
Can Refresh

And They All Can Refresh

There was a certain man and his son during ancient times
on their journey across the desert to the next town. They came upon
a river, watered, washed and tied their <u>donkey</u> to a tree. Sitting in the
shade under the tree, the boy noticed that all kinds of people were
there.
He saw the common people, whom we would call poor, the merchant
and the King, sitting under a tent with his servants. They were all
working together.

The young man asks, "Father how can all of these people that do not
associate with one another at home interact with each other now?"
The wise man looked at the young man, turned towards the men
smiling and said, "No matter how weak or poor, rich or mighty you
are, you still have to wash your Ass."

Just Like Rain

Just Like Rain

So softly the wetness touched my lips.
Overwhelmingly surprised,
i was excited to see it finally manifest itself to the world.
When i felt the moisture i didn't even touch it.;
i let it naturally stay on my body,
careful not to remove it from my presence.

This marks the start of a beautiful day.
Just like rain, joy and peacefulness poured over me.
Once again I felt the reality of myself ... Strong ... Alive.
Smiling within myself; I know the cycle will repeat, once
again come.

Can You Hula-Hoop Like This

Can You Hula-Hoop Like This

scented candles
thousand miles from the world
ours slow down as society rages on
midday rendezvous
playground memories as we collide
like teenagers at recess

can you hula-hoop like this she asks
body tight
ascending the pitchers mound smiling
catching my breath as 1 learn to hula-hoop like her
BUT SHE STAYS ON TOP

Glimpses Of A Dream

Glimpses Of a Dream

I will run up a horizontal plane
just to experience the depths and
circumference of your diamond circle
My mouth speaks volumes
about the flavors of the Diamond Circle Cafe'
I eat there often and the diamond circle is
always glad to see me come
your doors are open late and
I am a guest invited in

Climb the width and height
of the mountainous shaft of my being
to explore and drink in the sight
Your secret getaway of
an Islander's Paradise goes untold yet
the natives love to see you
bask and bathe in my cascading waterfall
and shower in the spray
Lay out like a beach as the thunderous tide
ebbs and flows

A Sunday Afternoon

A Sunday Afternoon

Slow down
Let me wash your hair

Not in the shower or tub
Faucets overpower the moment
Go'n back to old ways
Let me wash your hair

Warm water pitcher
Hints of chamomile lavender
Reggae jazz in the air
Let me wash your hair

Recline
strong hands massage
Rhythmic motions
Daylight gives way to candles
Let me wash your hair

Sundress falls
Glimpses I dare not touch
Breath quickens
Your entire being pleased
Let me wash your hair

A Fiddler's Song

A Fiddler's Song

I steal you away in the night
like thieves
entering your thoughts
like you wouldn't believe
being lead by the hum of the piper's pied
breaking the night mist in a gallop stride
colliding as one to the way we ride
slipping from my hands
in our thrusting ways
for these are just mere thoughts
in a daydreamed haze
until he meet
just keep your hum
pleasured within will surely
come

She Loves My Mouth

She Loves My Mouth

my mouth splits her womb stroking
giving verbal conception
to twins named thought and expression
birthing wisdom and truth
raised to the sky in honor like Roots
she loves my mouth

intertwined in a primal dance
as my mouth licks kisses and teases
behind ears thighs and places unknown
causing silent moans
exposing vulnerable thoughts of nakedness
that have been covered for so long
she loves my mouth

being blindfolded and bound
my tongue devours and discovers
secret places
the mask falls
while her being quakes erupts and explodes
screaming exotic expressions of becoming so free
she loves my mouth

A Shopping Spree

A Shopping Spree

Your breasts are my rising and my fall
curved line silhouette
conquering mountains outstretched hands
yearn to be touched
Feel my thoughts
don't MAKE me wait so long
Shapely figures remind me of you
peripheral peeps burn
clothing conceals the urgency of our flame
it's only ours to extinguish
you breathe upon me I melt
moments within your touch
I hear nothing
Hard to keep secrets are so sweet
"DAMN"
don't let our husbands find out

She Still Loves You

She Still Loves You

the reaction of the wind happens so fast
you were amazed
the blades of those windmills
move in timeless slow motion
bound up energy is released
everything in the path of the windmills
thrash around
as if an eerie poetry in motion
this is your first time hitting her
now do you feel like a man?

Behind Your Smiling Face

Behind Your Smiling Face

You are loving me with your lips
but each spoken word
sends me into another chase
hiding your pure deception
behind your smiling face

you honestly think that I don't understand
the control you enjoy
but just can't break free of the magnetism you employ
the remote is passed from person to person
sending me yet on another chase
hiding your pure deception
behind your smiling face

so the dance continues like a masquerade ball
spinning and twirling some day to fall
until I recognize who I am in dis-grace
please hide your pure deception
behind your smiling face

Masquerade Ball

Masquerade Ball

We stand face to face as we dance
You smile at me
Truly in your heart lives hatred
Angered, like a child
placing their fingers
on a frosted glass window
starting at one point
drawing a sad face

The mask is unveiled
but I don't lead on
We continue to dance

Melodic tones spin us into a frenzy
we cannot control the dance
I close my eyes
trying hard not to see the hoards of people
dancing and laughing behind their masks
(dancing so slowly)

When the music stops I open my eyes
hoping I'm all alone
We stand face to face and you smile at me

Pull Back The Curtain

Pull Back The Curtain

Let's count up the righteous
make us a list
spit in the wind
and it comes back
I turn my back on you
and words fly out of my mouth
at the speed of sound
connect
pull back the curtain

This is the world that you've created
creating phrases and thoughts
that make you cringe
cowardly sneaking by
coming out of the back door
pointing at me
you hate my guts
because I pulled back the curtain

Where do you go after your speech
who's in control
controlled by someone
even the ones bringing the world events
audition and read scripts
but when the news is off the cuff
there's a fist to cuff
pull back the curtain

As long as you are doing your dirt
sweeping it under the rug
smug
turning your back
on your wife that's flirt'n
I'll be there in the recesses
pulling back the curtain

Have you ever had
a pain that just wouldn't
go away?

Have you ever had a pain that just wouldn't go away?

shut up I'm not interested
when things are going well
you open your mouth
mess things up
take me off track
keep me from my goals

I'm tired of arguing with you
the conversation is too real
opening your mouth
causes hurt and pain

I stood listening
while you were glistening
having your moment in the sun
since your voice hinders my moves
I stumble when I run

I hate you
debate you
the more you talk
I get stronger

I Defeat My Opponent
In The Arena Of My Mind

I Defeat My Opponent
In The Arena Of My Mind

teeth cutting through my bottom lip
like a piercing
not even wiping the blood
anger canceled out the pain
swinging my fist at the target
landing every blow
fingers numb
swinging harder to adjust the sensation
of bringing my adversary down
I threw in some kicks too
beads of sweat popping
rage
the scene plays over before my eyes
all of this takes place in my mind
as I remain calm receiving the bad news

Some People Just Won't Stop Talking

Some People Just Won't Stop Talking

HUMMING BIRDS AND BUMBLE BEES
ARE ALL I SEE
NEVER RESTING NEVER NESTING
BUSY AS A BEE

HUMMING BIRDS AND BUMBLE BEES
ARE ALL I FEAR
SPENDING RESTLESS MINUTES BUZZING
IN MY EAR

HUMMING BIRDS AND BUMBLE BEES
ABOUT MY HEAD
DO YOU EVEN REMEMBER WHAT
YOU'VE JUST SAID

HUMMING BIRDS AND BUMBLE BEES ARE
ALL I SEE
GET SOME LIFE ABOUT YOURSELF AND
GET AWAY FROM ME

Unbound But Not Free

Unbound But Not Free

Young brother who are Langston Hughes
and Huey Newton
They're dead
Are we free
Yep

Then whom are we running from
every time you see a black man
He's running up a field or
around a track
only to come back
to where he started
unbound but not free

my brother then tell me of Malcolm X
and Martin Luther King Jr.
still dead
Freedom must be in sight
Huh

Then who are we bonding with
We have a million men marching
All the way to make bond
Only after X ing out their brother or spouse
On MLK blvd or in front of the dope house
Unbound but not free

Dispensing Thoughts
Between Time & Time

Dispensing Thoughts Between Time & Time

Successful people don't watch TV
They put down their remote and come see me
To close their eyes and look into mine
So I can open their minds
Shedding some beautiful light
While you sit around
Talking about this @#$% is tight
Reading line after line
Trying to see if I'm black or white
"His words are so strong
Radiant like sunshine"
But I'm only talking
Dispensing thoughts between time & time

Now That The Marching Is Over

Now That The Marching Is Over

Why should i express myself
when everyone is talking for me.
It took me 400 years to learn i had a mouth,
decades to learn i couldn't use it.
Now that i've learned i have a voice
i don't know what to say.
So, why should i express myself
when everyone is talking for me.

Paradigm

Paradigm

I have a lot to say yet no one listens so I write
look into my words are they a picture a movie a
reflection or a sight
its all in the way you see things that make them
wrong or right

MOUTHSWIDESHUT

MOUTHSWIDESHUT

Leaves falling in autumn wind...rubbing your shoulders...
                      Crisp breeze walking through the park
Smell that scent of wood smoke in the air
                             Memories of a far away place...
Metaphoric comfort you think my poems are

These lines shattering glass...
               Energy like Tupac, Public Enemy or Busta Rhymes
Guitars screaming... up close to the speakers... heavy metal
                          Twelve thousand screaming fans...

It's 120 on the highway...
                         Almost taking it off the road
Before snatching the wheel
                     SPLASH, cold water alarm clock...
The truth hurts leaving your mouthswideshut

Block Writers

day all
computer this at sitting from
hurts shoulder my
money the for it in I'm now
passion a as off started it
screen computer a or
paper at looking of sick

backspace
backspace
delete

week a now
days three been it's but
moment a as off started
vacuum a into sucked gets
connect to try I flow every
air-mid in suspended be to
seem just time

backspace
backspace
delete

top to bottom, left to right from reads it

Block Writers

The Baby

The 'Baby'

last night I had a baby
sheer pain sweat and tears
went the length of the night
the sensation didn't hit me all at once
it started earlier in the day
getting stronger and stronger
until it was time for the baby to be born
as the baby crowned and came out
I was the one agonizing and screaming
while the baby lays there peaceful

Tyrant Like Him

Tyrant Like Him

I've been at war since 1970.
My enemy knows me better than I know myself.
Standing in the corners
peeping at me when I'm looking in the mirror.
We both have studied our target.
No inspection, no UN vote, just BAM!
An attack so violent
it can't even be seen on TV.
Massive casualties.
We'll cry for them later.

I decided to strike first.
Kicked a battle off that would last for decades.
I try my best to kill my enemy.
Can't see em
because he's clean, cunning.
An operation so covert,
its awesomely private.
The world around us doesn't even know the war exists.
That doesn't stop the carnage.

Grasping in the darkened mist
trying to break its neck.
It quietly continues.
(as a whisper)
Like I said; you can't see this on TV.

The Day Summer Died

The Day Summer Died

Now that I look back
Summertime was you
Working
Tending the garden
Taking care of the dawgs
Cutting the grass
I tried to follow you everywhere
'Till you ran me back home
"I want to whoop you so bad
My stomach hurts"

You gave me my first job
Cranking the mower
Running to Snipes
To get your RC
"Make A's Now"

Hands strong enough to work all day
Gentle enough to teach me to shave
I used to hate the way that shaving powder smelled
"Granddaddy why you using a knife?"
Still would sneak back later
To try and do what you just did
Not even knowing you took the blade out
So I wouldn't cut myself
You knew I was coming back

I walked in my Daddy's and Your shoes
Just to be like you
All those things you quietly taught me
Molded me into who I am now
I'll try to be a big boy
And be as strong as you
  "Make A's Now"

Oh How Sweet
The Voices Within

Oh How Sweet The Voices Within

Voices now give way to vision
so now I see what they are saying
the silvery blue scene vibrates and comes into view
with a reel of tape starting up like an old projector
the voices in my head are now showing me rolls and
rolls of film
locking me away in a dimly lit dingy theater
not even gracious enough to offer me popcorn or
a soda

I am asleep but reality begins
Oh how sweet the voices within

Even with my eyes covered and closed
I can still see the raw footage
of my present past to come
piercing and penetrating my being unwilled
the volume is damn near mute yet thunder in my ears
I let out a blood curdling scream
hoping someone would hear me
and shake me free from this awful night out

I am asleep but reality begins
Oh how sweet the voices within

dressed in my best suit shoes buffed shirt crisp
do I deserve this theater ticket for one
thinking
is it just me
I scramble to look around this musty room
to see if there are other onlookers
to no avail

I am asleep...

therearenogoodmornings

therearenogoodmornings

Lightly sleeping
cotton tumbling on carpet is maddening
and waking up every three hours is getting old
and the lines in my eyes and face look like a road map

I sprang up when a light wind hit my face
was that a nuzzle or the sounds of waking
making me sit up at the crack of dawn
running cracking my toe on the dresser

Folgers' didn't wake me up
and why do they make those commercials
with families waking up to the sound of music
and birds chirping with dronelike smiles on their faces

but in my house
gale force winds toss me yet I hold on to the bed
anchoring for safety while the current of these superfluous waves
spin me into sporadic rituals

now little ones are screaming
because they are caught up in this chaotic flow
only adding more energy to this whirlwind
but neglecting self I do all I can to protect and comfort my kids

as the morning's tropical wind subsides
not hearing a sound you lay sleeping
like a bygone prophet in the bottom of a storm tossed boat
you walk in with a giant smile beaming
good morning
I glare

Reflections:
What are you looking at?

Reflections:
What are you looking at?

YOU LAUGH IN THE FACE OF DANGER
.......HA.......HA.......HA

YOU'RE LOOKING IN A MIRROR

2Cups Away
From A Headache

2Cups Away From A Headache

cool damp wet
tall round
abundant empty
abundant many
harsh deafening quiet
rapid thundering
morning night
full happy embarrassed
stupid romantic
holy weak brilliant
capable vulnerable
somebody help me

And To An Empty Audience I Bow

And To An Empty Audience I Bow

It's a celebration and everyone is invited
A culmination of my life's work is being honored tonight
And it is going to be a party
Everyone is making it such a big to do
Even though my work is stuff I love to do
Tuxes and Gowns, Limos
Hard work, blood, sweat and tears do pay off
They haven't thrown a hand full of dirt in my face yet
And I am just getting started

When the moment of truth
to receive my well wishes is now
I take my due humble with pride
And to an empty audience I bow.

The Finish Line

The Finish Line

pushing
shoving
coming through the crowd at record speed
like a fullback
finding a crease to run through
to sprint to the goal line
legs flexed
rippling

everyone is on their own pace
yet you run to that gaping hole
that hole that will hold you in slumber
life blurs as you turn your head
to see the next opportunity
to pass the slowest one in your path
you missed it

no one tried to tackle
the person in the business suit and track shoes
but will throw dirt on your face
when you dive into the finish line

The Place Of My
Childhood

The Place Of My Childhood

On my way home
I turned down a street
long forgotten
The place of my childhood

Turning past the tree
I neared the house
Didn't realize
I still had the key to get in

Coming upon the abandoned house
comforting memories entered my head
I'm home again

I walked around like a kid in my youth
Even went to the backyard
Where we played ball
I forgot how good it felt being here

Reaching my hand toward the knob
Of the room I grew up in
My heart pounded in my throat
Almost afraid to go in

Could I handle what was waiting for me
Behind the door-------
-------Hands trembling as I turned the knob
exhaled and walked away

Always Resist Temptations

The Nazarite Vow

The Nazarite Vow

You watch them grow one by one
so big and strong.
Grooming, keeping them from harm or danger.
The loved ones being a reflection of you
bring glory to your Head.

Nothing could prepare you for this.
Guillotine cuts so swift causes such pain.
Longing for those you nurtured from infancy.
Gone.

Darkness days,
Rubbing your hands through your head.
Where could they have gone?
Left lonely;
you can't stop living though.

Remember the vow you made.
Raise them, let them go.
That's right.
Obedience,
Being obedient is the key to having more.
Lock em, bond, keep them close to your heart.
That is what brings the Glorious.
Keep your promises though.

Educational Bulimia

Educational Bulimia

I saw you as I walked in sitting at the table
all kinds of smells and flavors were in the air
It was hard not to take it all in
With my nose
My eyes
Then something caught my eye
And I couldn't believe my eyes
You were just sitting there
Eating and eating
Feeding and gorging yourself
With such a small frame
I strained myself
To see how were you taking it all in
In a matter of time you were stuffed
Stuffed to the gills you could just pop
Then POP
I knew it wouldn't be long till all you'd consumed
came spewing out of your mouth
To everyone's gaping amaze

Are we getting smarter
Seems like we are only taught
To study to pass a test
When the test is to
Never never never stop discovering

Circle Of Chairs

Circle Of Chairs

I was quietly sitting watching a game
the game goes like this
there are a circle of chairs
and a group of kids
the kids usually out number
the circle of chairs
as the music starts the players walk around
the circle of chairs

when the music stops
at random
the players quickly move to an empty seat
leaving one child standing
because they were not quick enough to find an
empty chair
sadly the child walks to the side
waiting until another game begins
watching as the other children are defeated
by the circle of chairs

Is this just a game or a cruel imitation of life?
the circle of chairs

Someone Asked Me, What Is Leadership?

Someone Asked Me, What Is Leadership?

A cry pierced the blackness
Which way do we go?
I thought long and hard
About the direction we should take
Suggestions roared
From the ones who trusted me
Destiny waits

Sweat beads
Heart pounding
One hasty rash movement
Would send us into the abyss

Gathering myself
With calming thoughts
I remembered the tools
The tools I've been trained with
Then
I realized
I have to take the first step

1 Only Asked For Forgiveness

l Only Asked For Forgiveness

Balled up in a fetal position
l could still taste the stench in my mouth
when l uttered "forgive me".
"The truth shall set you free"
(we were so precisely taught) echoed in my head.
Nothing or no one but the Creator could help me escape
the black gloved hand that will devour any open flesh.
l heard the Just Judge thunder, "No more than 40 stripes".
The judgment was set.

The painful reality of the hot leather strap cutting my face,
cleansed my mouth.
The wrath of the strap caused my flesh to split open.
Every secret sin and transgression oozed out of me
like a stream of lava.
It's funny how pain escapes you in traumatic situations.
The only pain l felt was deep within my soul.

Falling to the cool dirt, my sentence was served.
No one ever said forgiveness doesn't come with punishment
or correction.
Within an inch of my life, l finally learn
the sweetness of true forgiveness.
The one who gave the punishment, sparing my life
helped me from the ground.
The sky is so radiantly blue, so clear.

Don't Take Things
For Granted

Don't Take Things For Granted

you seem to find me every day about this time
going out of your way to be noticed
sometimes i don't realize that you are there

i take it for granted that I'll see you
yet long for you when things around me grow dark
nothing works when you are not around

chaos reigns in your absence
Everything in disorder
i guess that's why the Creator made you first

you're the only thing in my life that stays constant
when everything else changes keeping your course
staying firm to your charge and what you were founded
on we all can learn from you

Laugh Like A Child

Laugh Like A Child

Remember
It used to take two people
To fold a bed sheet
It used to bring us closer together
Like a dance
A ballroom dance
Step one fold
Step two return
Arms stretched out wide
Eager to meet your partners return
Arms in tight one
Arms out wide two
Remember

Statistic

Statistic

I was born a statistic
a ransom was put on my head at birth
three major operations by the age of 19
the odds were against me since day one

I've slipped through death's grip many times
I didn't even think I would make it past high school
I was told I wouldn't make it to 21
people around me didn't realize
I was living in the scope of an assassin
I put everyone around me in danger
stayed up late nights
fearing I would take my last breath while I slumbered

as the sunlight hit my eyes
I woke up next to my wife and unborn child
getting prepared for the day in my new career
I'm 33 years old
I was born a statistic

Return Of Kings

Return Of Kings

Did you know that you are descendants of kings?
Groping around like darkness at noon day
Misdirected in a country that you built
Getting irate when someone calls you out
And reminds you of your quest
Descendant of Kings
Feverishly trying to put a round peg in a square hole
Spent wasted years fighting
When I should have been perfecting what's mine
Eat what's yours and get full
Before you reach for someone else's

Show us the exit to get back to where we came from
Better yet a one-way ticket
Just like the luxury cruises we first took
To the Bahamas or Florida keys
We have keys but we are driving around in circles
Looking at how they say we should live
Speeding off after we've told granddad and
them to shut up
Descendant did you know you are of kings
One day I woke up and saw that I was black
So if I walk around like royalty forgive me
I'm a descendant of KINGS

When The Cards
Are Laid

When The Cards Are Laid

my thoughts wander like circlets of smoke
sacrificing themselves
off the tip of an expensive cigar
whipping around the room
teasing the senses of the crowd
surrounding an intense game of Black Jack
sunglasses make it hard to see what I am thinking
but many will witness my rise or fall
when the cards are laid

life doesn't cut to commercial
but keeps rolling
menacing
mimicking like a 24 hr news channel
sensational top stories break in
on the numbing randomness
a young heiress' prison break attempt
and her childish antics of realizing that
She is human
as the crowd's head turned
I turned the Ace

Footrace

Footrace

There was a fellow who asked me one day
Was I working out for power
Or bodybuilding competition
And I told him no
I just wanted to be healthy

Then I thought about it
I am competing
In a foot race
Not against a clock but time

Trying to make it to life's finish line
Before death catches up with me

Today 1 Met Me

Today I Met Me

Just smile and wave
I checked the mirror three times
and made sure my shirt was tucked in just right
the lines in my face and circles around my eyes
reveal that I have been up since five
this morning
with the alarm blaring in my ears
and the snooze button halfway missing
from the constant morning impact
of a person constantly trying to get his grind on
spending hours and days surfing the net
reading the right book
the right magazine
checking the right text message
on the right phone checking the right email
on the right notebook computer
with the right shit-eating grin on my face
in front of just the right person
drinking the right cup of coffee
in the right coffee house
on the right block
on the suggestions of someone else
to insure the come up
you see
these are just ramblings of a man fed up
with what is
and the reality of what he allowed himself to be
becoming lost in the expectations of others
and what he thought to make himself free
in the cloud of clutter and chaos
and the appointments of people to see
a wise man gave me a nugget of wisdom
and today I met me

Kundalini

Kundalini

I'm not a Poet
I'm a Prophet with a rhythmic line scheme
Coming across in my journey Poets with a scheme
To rhyme for a profit

Telling me my craft is to sell books and CD's
When these
Souls we encounter hunger
For wisdom and knowledge
Looking for ways
Many days to turn their lives around
And when you are called to the stage
You throw down
But can't be found
When the curtains come down
We're playing

We're playing
When one word from our anointed mouths
Can plant a vision into someone's being
Till begin
Being
Becomes
Yet we sit and talk shit
About another Prophet's line spit
His flows
His moans
His hums

I'm not a Poet I'm a Prophet
with a rhythmic line scheme
Coming across in my journey Poets with a scheme
To rhyme for a profit

Boasting that he isn't you
Yet conflicted in thought
Because somehow he sells
More books and CD's than you
Without reciting a three or four minute piece
You marvel at his release
When he turns to address
The four winds of the earth
From which the voices cry peace
They cry peace ...
... We're playing

About The Author

Quiethouse Poet, Kolayah-KeeVan was born KeeVan Barnard Wilson. This award winning poet is a published author and founder of Quiethouse Culturetainment, Host of OneVoice Radio [www.blogtalk.com/onevoice] Words Cafe' Live Starbucks and The Gnu's Room Bookstore of Auburn/Opelika and Poetry@Taina's Art Gallery of Montgomery, an empowerment speaker, a member of Auburn Art Association, Culturetainer, Fitness Expert and Lifestyle Performance Coach.

Kolayah has performed on many stages. He has been a featured speaker at major Universities and Community Colleges, at Alabama Shakespeare Festival's CultureFest, Wellness Workshops, Fitness Forums and at Churches.

When he is not transforming your mind with his awesome work with a pen or voice, he is coaching his clients in transforming their bodies and well being as the Owner/Trainer of REDDLION Fitness [Re Defining Destiny Living In Oneness].

Promoting literature and art is a joy for Kolayah and he has been Active in this effort for many years. Kolayah feels the need to revive the art of poetry, spoken word, storytelling, self expression and enlightenment in his community and surrounding areas.

Acknowledgements

I would like to thank Yahweh, Creator of all, my family, loved ones and fans. To Abiyah, for your unmatched support. Ebony Flake, you are the first Poet and friend to believe in and take part in my vision of advocating Literary Art, and the first Poet that I ever read for and performed with. Shan, girl you always come through in the clutch and your poetic skills are developing as you grow and become. DJ Woodgrain, man you brought an awesome vibe to our shows, much success to you in your desires. Joi Miner your poetry is beauty, thanks for traveling the highways promoting and performing for yourself as well as Quiethouse. Thanks to Trish Toomer (Toomers Coffee Co.) for enjoying my passion and providing your coffee shop to kick off my career in performing poetry and literary art. Kenny and Karina Polen-Davis (Taina's Art Gallery, Montgomery, AL), you have a great vision for bringing back the culture into our community and making The Poetry Lounge a monthly event. Your vibe and love for visual and performing art is outstanding. Katie (Starbucks Opelika, AL) you have an awesome place that helps the Literary Lounge Cafe' to come alive. Your inspiring words Tan bring calmness to Chaos. Shaun Judah, thank you for taking time out of your busy career to review and forward this body of work, for being a prophet and an encouragement to many. When we first met you felt like family to me. Jahbu Ourinde; you breathe life into poetry and spoken word, thank you for all of those talks that we had and for teaching me the true spirit of Performance Poetry. I found my voice. Eve Kneeland, thank you for being an educator and expanding developing minds. Eryk Moore, Nabraska, Star Lisa; Much love FAM, you have traveled many times from Atlanta to The Literary Lounge Cafe' and The Poetry Lounge to share your Calling of sparking the soul and mind with your spoken word and have given me a charge to continue being a voice and creating the platform for others to be heard.

Acknowledgements

Thanks to The Gnu's Room Bookstore and Hastings Bookstore for shelving and SELLING my books. Much love to all the lovers and fans of poetry and my work. Your continued support helps to bring a stronger awareness of Literary Art and that lets me know that if you create and produce something good, people will buy it and come out to support it.
Thank You.

More from Quiethouse Publishing

To book Kolayah for poetry readings, spoken word events, adult literacy groups, youth and young adult empowerment groups, seminars, expos and workshops contact LaShawn Wilson at 334.707.2296 www.myspace.comquiethouseculturetainment.

To order a copy of MOUTHSWIDESHUT (2007 Quiethouse Publishing), and/ or Only 1 Will Speak (2008 Quiethouse)
go to www.lulu.com/quiethouse or www.myspace.com/kolayah

"Reserve a copy of; The Becoming, NOW...!"